I Have a Name

WESLEYAN POETRY

DAVID IGNATOW

I Have a Name

Wesleyan University Press

PUBLISHED BY UNIVERSITY PRESS OF NEW ENGLAND

HANOVER AND LONDON

Wesleyan University Press

University Press of New England, Hanover, NH 03755

© 1996 by Wesleyan University

All rights reserved

Printed in the United States of America

5 4 3 2 1

CIP data appear at the end of the book

ACKNOWLEDGMENTS DUE: *Black Moon, Black Warrior, Boulevard, Caliban, Doubletake,* E. L. F. Associates, *Forkroads, Grand Street, Hanging Loose, The Nation, New England Review,* New Rivers Press, *North Stone Review, Ohio Review, Ontario Review, Pivot, Plum Review, Poetry, The Prose Poem, Verse, Virginia Quarterly Review.*

The publisher gratefully acknowledges the support of Lannan Foundation in the publication of this book.

For
Jerome Mazzaro
Ralph Mills
Virginia R. Terris

Contents

SECTION ONE

SECTION TWO

SECTION THREE

SECTION FOUR

SECTION ONE

It's a Sick Life

being poet. He writes
to give himself health
so long as he writes.
When he lays down his pen
or shuts off his typewriter
he falls ill again.

He finds himself in the world, bare,
except that he hears the poetry
of gunfire and cries of revenge,
worse yet, of murder.

It is poetry he could translate
into words, if gripped by despair,
the words forming a burial chant
for the dead and those crazed
by gunfire.

Poetry lifts away
from its origin, so as
to maintain itself, so as
to speak, so as
to cure itself
of death and of life.

What Is This Life, Anyway

finding in death an inspiration
to live or seek to live
among the flashing guns
and yes, because many are born
amid carnage, persisting
in wanting to live, to give birth.

What do they know—
that it's beautiful to die,
which keeps them at it
generation after generation?

Do they see death beautiful,
to live to see themselves
murdered or as murderers?

And I, pen in hand,
praise life,
its capacity for praise.

As If

The prayerful humanity of Bach,
the soldier machinegunning—
I don't know how to reconcile
one with the other and to the living,
where with others I walk, stunned.

In a cafe music is pouring itself
in joy for itself for anyone to dream
of reconciliation with conflicted life.
Farther down the road an energetic man
is beating his wife.

How to live in confusion
and as skeptic, angry
to have been born to music
and to screams intermingling,
as if—not one without the other—
to make a whole of it.

We Have Bodies

to make palpable the bitter
and the beautiful
to make our being worth to us,
beautiful and bitter.

The Butcher Shop

a disciplined institution
of slaughter allows pigs, chickens,
rabbits and all other animals
on the chopping block
for your benefit and perpetuation.

It's slaughter among ourselves
that is nerve wracking.

In the butcher shop, slaughter is exempt
by its civility.

Nothing further need be said.
You hear the intonation of price,
weight, packaging and "Have a nice day."
A feeling of accomplishment
before a block of wood,
a kind of altar.

Since Then

I am in search of revival,
entering living rooms,
kitchens and bedrooms
in search of a beginning.

Since then, I have had nothing
to say, inwardly silent,
sun warming me to write:
what I am left to do.

The Center of Gravity

is in speaking of silences about living
that cannot be spoken, dense with unhappiness—
such a silence that speaks to the density
of living

I Am Alone as I Write

yet writing this places me
within the society of others
who, acknowledging it or not,
enact my solitude. But having said
it sets me apart in a silent community
turned in on itself,
away from truth.
We cannot act by truth.
It is not life.

I've Nothing to Offer

but forgiveness
for the cruelty of the impersonal
in myself. I have not been
my own vision of kindness.

Still, I must forgive myself
if I am to forgive others,
none of us happy with ourselves,
of earth, air and water.

Long Island

As cars drive by on Southern State Parkway,
a community of trees lines up alongside
each other for miles, branches intertwined.

The cars speed by, a community in themselves,
speeding apart.

The Ward

The ward attendant who owns his home speaks amicably with patients. They come to him with requests, and he treats these requests respectfully. They cannot be fulfilled, because out of the ordinary. He does not say so explicitly. It is not necessary to insult by flaunting their illness. It is enough to say, "It's really not done," and they walk off to continue playing pool. Patients and attendant compose the ward.

Observed

Reality is the other person.
We are all imagination
on whom the other intrudes
to give us pain and sorrow
of our unfulfillment
in the other.

The Restaurant

The restaurant I walk into expects me to have the cash or credit card, and the waiter expects to be tipped, and I expect to be served a meal that will satisfy me gastronomically and aesthetically. With all these requirements fulfilled, we'll feel a brotherliness among ourselves. We'll smile at one another and perhaps exchange a joke in revelation of our oneness, demonstrating it in this small but significant manner.

Here, alas, is the sadness beneath the surface: I walk in without my credit card or cash, yet seat myself to eat, demanding the best in the house. Later, I report that I am without cash or credit card and have eaten out of hunger. The waiter, the restaurant owner, the chef come together at my table with the great compassion that one who is hungry has come to them to be saved, a compliment to our brotherhood. But this is a dream. Still, what I dream is a kind of existence. Is it possible that if I did live the dream, I would dream of division in me for excitement, combat, power and domination?

Moths

He sees one fluttering around the room and, concerned for his woolen suits in the closet, he hunts it down. It lands on his desk. He slams his hand down. Not quite finished wiping his hand of the remains, he sees yet another and knows then that there must be a nest in one corner. Methodically, he goes about killing this nest when, sure enough, he discovers a colony above his kitchen stove. He kills them all, to his satisfaction, and as he lies down on his bed, his head propped upon a pillow to entertain himself with TV, a stream of moths pours out of a tiny hole in the baseboard just above the hot water pipe.

By god, he is angry and jumps out of bed and finds a rag to plug the hole. It fits perfectly and stops the stream, and, oh god, as he looks to assure himself, he sees them coming through by the hundreds. His room is filled with them, on his shoulders, head, arms, legs and face. He can hardly breathe. He rushes to the street door for air, and as he opens the door a new cloud pours in from the woods. He is covered from head to feet in a gray flutter of wings, like a winged creature. He is choking on the moths crawling up his nose, into his ears, into his eyes. They penetrate his clothes to his bare skin: chest, legs, groin. They are penetrating his penis and are crawling up into his anus.

He is their victim. He is their prey. They are relentless, busy, and he is weighed down by layers upon layers, forcing him to his knees. He cannot scream. They fill his mouth, his throat, in horror. He last remembers dying of lack of air, lying stretched out upon the floor beneath silent, gray outspread wings.

The Man Who Fell Apart in the Street
as He Walked

First, his right arm swung loose and dropped to the sidewalk. He walked on, not bothering to look back at the arm lying at right angles to itself. People stopped to stare down at it. One woman, horrified, screamed out to him that he had lost his right arm. "Come back and pick it up." He walked on.

His left arm began to dangle dangerously, and that too fell to the sidewalk. He continued walking, when suddenly he paused, acting as if crippled from the waist down, and sank to the concrete. His left leg swaying beneath him had fallen away. He landed on his back, one leg clinging to his waist. But now he felt it necessary to speak, a crowd gathered around him. "I've been expecting this. It is possible that if you bring me my arms and leg I will find a way to attach them. It has happened before." The crowd was unbelieving, angry. It was as if he were mocking them, worse, being contemptuous of them, with jobs to go to and errands to fulfill, not to mention family obligations for which they worked tirelessly—he made it all seem as if it were some kind of farce, casual as that. In the crowd, a man and woman were muttering between them angrily. They picked up his arms and leg and walked off with them. That would show him he could not make fun of them and get away with it.

At Table

People gorging on what is placed
before them. It could be their neighbor's heart,
but it is food of the day:
this grief adapted to survival
as the more thoughtful way.

Nobody knows for sure the reason.
Why not surviving others,
or, to be noble about it,
to celebrate that life consists
in overcoming our distaste for it,
taking it into our mouths
and swallowing, affirming our unity
with the living.

SECTION TWO

Lives

Bessie's face lingers before me,
as if to be touched, recalling
her life. A child, she does not
yet know, nor do I, her age.
She is standing at the door
of her parents' apartment together
with her mother to see my mother
and me off after a visit.

Bessie is eager to do well as a pianist,
her mother standing staunchly at her side.

❦

I see Bessie in her hardware store,
hauling barrels and crates
from off the truck and swearing
at her invalid husband. She curses
her father to whom she owes this life.
There is no piano, no practicing.
She is signing receipts for goods delivered
with stiff, coarsened fingers.

This is better, she will say viciously
to her husband, rather than to beg money
from her father and be refused. She
has taken on the hardware store
at his retirement to prove to him
she too can make money, lots of it,

at the same work. In spite,
she has married a sick man.

Bessie, going back into the store,
upbraids her husband for not overseeing
the shipment. He reminds her
of her father keeping his distance,
paying for the piano lessons
but refusing her money for clothes,
letting the woman fester in her want.

꘏

She has played Chopin for mother and me
and now we stand at the door
to say goodnight. Bessie
at her mother's side, as together
we begin to leave, my mother first
having praised Bessie,
echoing my pleasure.

Denied

What I'm living with is my father
striking my mother in the face.
My mother was stunned, holding her hand
to her face, unbelieving. That is the scene
I remember, as if it could set me straight
on the path to truth.

I know I do not forgive him.
I sit here thinking about it,
unable to get it out of mind,
not wanting to—that I wonder at,
but it is what I know
to have to take it in stride
and be the person to myself
founded on this episode.
Was this the life between them?

How would I have known,
as a youth seated
in the living room in sight
of the kitchen and thinking
my thoughts of sex, ambition
and friendships, hearing
from the kitchen a slap
upon my mother's face.
It was she I turned to
to confide in. I was humiliated.

My father too I loved
but was now filled with horror
for him and myself, he with whom
I would walk to visit relatives,
taking pride at being at his shoulder,
an equal in companionship
in silence between us
as we walked.

Bent over my typewriter,
I recall that months later
to ease my sense of grief,
I reminded them of the event,
seeking an explanation, and both
simultaneously denied the slap.

The Hebrew Lesson

What I remember is the rabbi's hand
upon my genitals to show what he meant
by ancient Hebrews taking an oath
of faithfulness in God.

I was surprised,
then offended
and then curious
that he should trouble himself,
he a rabbi, a man of learning
and soul, to place his hand
upon the parts from which I urinated.
I was awakened to a double standard
in the role of rabbi.

I was confused.
Did I have to learn from books
when already I knew of being
that I did not know until then?
What then, was superior:
book learning, intellect and soul
or the life and actions
originating in my genitals?

From then on I took my learning lightly,
instead guarding my genitals,
made aware of their sacredness,
of their threat to my body and life,
inhering in an oath.

From then on, when the rabbi came to teach,
I was alert to the movement of his hands.
My genitals were mine to guard,
to keep secure
as a sacred trust
conferred on me.

I was suspicious that he wished
the sacredness of my parts
to be in his possession. Eventually,
I saw less of him,
finally, not at all,
and it never was explained to me.

Adolescence

When I was a child I loved my bed
because of the dream of living
alone in the world with one girl
after everyone else, boys, I mean,
had been vanquished—by whom?
There had to be a catastrophe.
I was not strong enough,
nor as bright as the others
to kill them off.

With the blanket enfolding me,
the room mine exclusively,
I had a door I could close,
exactly as I would close out
competition for my girl.

I was not sure of myself
in the competition for love
in the street and in school
where we met. A boy of my age
and a girl in class would stand
together and talk as a couple,
like those I would see in the street
walking side by side, grown-up.

In the classroom, girls would approach me
too, but I would fail to speak.
What I should have said in my shyness,
which did not allow me to speak—

at least of the obvious, politely:
that the teacher was nice,
that I liked the course: topics
I overheard chatted about.
I could not talk, a girl before me,
the very one with whom I dreamt
of living alone with in the world,
offering herself in my dream.
I was not about to tell her in class
that we were alone in the world,
that rivals had been vanquished
by me.

I sat down in my seat, leaving her
to walk away in silence to her seat.

What could I learn from my mother
that would help me with a girl?
I studied her at her housework.
I studied her in conversation
with my dad. I studied my dad talking
and gesturing, raising and lowering
his voice, heard him speak of family matters
and of finances, his voice and his posture
varying with the subject, as he talked,
my mother listening. I studied
the conversation between guests, especially
that of the women talking to the men,
the men replying, the women answering,
each couple with an air of belonging
together at that moment exclusively,
as I had dreamt in bed but in classroom
had failed.

It was possible it could be done,
one day at their age, with double chins
and stiff legs as they walked. In
their chairs they crossed their legs
slowly, as in pain of age.

But they were not successful either,
grown old, leaving behind the pleasures
they must have known in youth. It was
failure for them too, and so I sat
commiserating silently,
enjoying their company of resigned speech
and bodies. I was one with them
and knew I would be able to speak
with a girl out of this new advanced age
I had taken on in resignation
at failure in the end. I would speak
as a wisened child, knowing how my dream
would end: that life was bracketed
between a dream and a defeat.

I Was an Angry Man

when first we met.
And you, did you love me
to make love your life?
I did and I was impatient
with it. Were you?

Love now has no other cause
but to point to our mistakes.
It departed, leaving
two persons looking
at each other
in the hollow of their home.

Listening

You wept in your mother's arms
and I knew that from then on
I was to forget myself.

Listening to your sobs,
I was resolved against my will
to do well by us
and so I said, without thinking,
in great panic, To do wrong
in one's own judgment,
though others thrive by it,
is the right road to blessedness.
Not to submit to error
is in itself wrong
and pride.

Standing beside you,
I took an oath
to make your life simpler
by complicating mine
and what I always thought
would happen did:
I was lifted up in joy.

I Have Already Written You Off

You have become a subject to write about.
I write with ease
because you no longer are real to me,
but the person I have conceived
in my imagination

You will not knock on my door
to tell me what I already know
of your opinion of me. You have become
the poem: friendly,
forgiving. It is worth having,
it fulfills a need in the streets
and rooms of the life we led
to which I offer a poem
in recompense for the failure
between us.

Asleep

I am abandoned to a dream,
in the desert: she is
rounded and statuesque,
the color of sand. The heat
of the sun has drawn her up
into form.

At dusk, as I lie down
exhausted in the heat,
her arms, legs, breasts,
face and belly crumble
to the desert floor.

Each sunrise I meet her figure
rising up from the sand,
tempting me to kiss her
and die of thirst.

I plod ahead
in search of an oasis,
if one can be detected
and not a mirage
in the sun's glare,
as she glides at my side.

A Man of His Time

He was riding the train away from her with whom he had just made love and was returning to his hotel room to take up his routine of work, and phone calls to his wife and child. No one on the train knew him. With them, he could feel no guilt. No one at the hotel knew him either. He was coming from an experience which might as well never have happened.

The train would carry him to any destination. The conductor would punch his ticket and passengers would sit alongside him, without enquiring or appealing to him to speak. He was what is called free. His newspaper headlines told of the death of thousands poisoned. He felt no guilt at that either.

One Can

One can fall in love as often as a tree grows leaves.
It is perfectly natural but not free of guilt
and complications, unless one takes oneself to be a tree.

Living

My routine existence: bed at eleven, up at six, breakfast
at seven, and so forth. Totally without inventiveness.
That's it. To have a peaceful life, live by routine. Speak
of that in wonder to others. They do not even know when
they will die. They cannot make dying a routine occurrence.

See them sort out the clothes they wish to buy from sales
racks to dress their bodies. See them fall back into the
routine of eating, sleeping, working and being who they are.
See the progress they make toward accepting their death by
living for the bargains and the large stock gains and the
relationship with one another to whom they expose their bodies
with their weaknesses and needs. But sympathy is not enough.
They ask for love. They ask for what death cannot provide.
They ask for what does not exist routinely.

A Name

What was it like for sociability
in the concentration camp? Did you talk
casually with your keeper,
who kept a revolver in his belt?
Joke with him who joked about turning you
into ashes? All the inmates were lying dead
of starvation or too weak to converse. For you,
he had human dimension, he could return
your conversation, even as he dragged you
to the crematorium to give humanity
a name.

For Ernest Lubin

You were shot in the back.
What can I say?
You knew the world.
You were not reluctant
to meet it. You did
pretty well: two children,
a job, an accomplished wife
and large apartment. I'd say
you were civilized.

Perhaps the killer could not
face your kindness, your speech
gentle as you refused him
the cash from your paycheck
in your pocket. You were arriving
home to share it with your family
and landlord. You may have said
as much candidly.

It is how you spoke with others
of whom you expected and received
a like response, and so you were firm,
each friend determined to care for his own
first, as he, who stood before you,
surely, as a man, would understand.

With courteous nod, you turned
to face the house elevator
and were shot, the back anonymous
at which the killer could allow himself
to fire.

This poem must end
in silence of one dead,
who probably in dying,
had he faced the killer,
would have apologized
for having caused the gun
to be fired.

I'm Not One

I'm not one you want to know
for long, dark to myself,
your eyes worried
to be with me, growing dark
to yourself in my shadow.

Addendum

It'll surely be eight o'clock,
however I wait for it,
and then at eight I can prepare
for ten arriving, whether I live
for it or accidentally die. What
am I then, if not important
to my hours?

SECTION THREE

A Brief Biog

Begin from the vacant.
A room unoccupied
I had forgotten
having left to visit
other rooms elsewhere
to adventure. I am back
in mind to this room.
It contains my childhood
where I sat and listened
to voices of my elders
who sat in leather chairs
and talked.

I listened, enthralled with life
for having induced such stories
I too wanted to tell,
hard, complicated, sometimes funny,
of pith, of magnitude, of accomplishment
and resignation, finally to become
the person seated in such a room
as this to tell the story
and be content that it would come
to telling in a room with others
with whom to share a falling short,
to be constrained to telling.
I listened and was curious
that one could talk of failure
with passion, as if to talk
was in itself success.

I became respectful of speech,
I could expect to speak
with that same authority
as could my elders and learn
to give my troubles my respect
for giving me the means
with which to exercise my satisfaction
in speaking to my peers who then
would speak to me in turn
with equal force of having lived:
a gathering as a child I sat
and listened to: a round of happenings
I learned to care about.

Dear Robert

Your roses are blooming in a basket
hung on the rail of my deck. I water them
each morning and wait for rain to take over,
if possible, but I enjoy the job, something
new to me who have been growing books,
fleurs du mal mainly.

Did you intend by these miniature roses
as a gift on my eightieth birthday
that I could look forward to beauty
and abundance in my life? The flowers
never cease to rise out of the buds.
Where one rose fades, another rises
to take its place. It falls to the deck
but to be admired and enjoyed, so long
as it's the rose and only the rose
that is red as blood upon the deck.

But what is this plant saying, as I believe,
in your hidden message—that I am destined
to live the rest of my life among roses
and that my life will give way to yet another
life on the stem of my poems, their roots
deep in the soil of my being, that poems will
emerge from poems read and laid aside,
giving birth to yet others in my absence?
I hope so. Why else would I have wanted
to continue as I was living, in crisis?

You know, you know very clearly, as only is
possible in sympathy, because like mine
your life has its peculiar context: dark father,
pallid mother and a limitless horizon
of earth and sky from which nothing arose
to guide you on to a path. War brought you
to recognize that to live meant
that under all and any circumstance
not to submit.

You grew your poems of love and death.
The roses you sent are flowers
of your effort to sustain yourself,
to tell me I too have survived.
Flowers are the compliment to give
each other and to enjoy, to attend a rose
in its receptive soil.

For Stanley Kunitz

I study your photo
at age three. You
are not smiling
and I look
at your not smiling
remembering
my photo as a child,
smiling, seated,
arms outspread
towards both arms of the chair
as on a cross, pleased,
it seems, with what is
going on with me, but you
are yet observing, not yet
ready to decide.

Here we are
into our years,
your face a plum of pleasure,
beaming. It makes me smile,
you free of yourself,
the past reordered,
victory for us
who serve life.

Wherever

Wherever I go,
into food stores,
into the john to piss,
I am haunted by the poem
yet to be written,
that I may live as a poem
when I die as a man.

What does he want of himself?
How to write without reservation,
yet without repugnance,
so that to value writing—
teeth, tongue, and terror—
he will accept the terror.

On Poetry

I'm tired of living.
I can't make poetry of misery.
Misery won't lift itself
to words.

Speaking about it takes a small, moderate effort—
not surprised but awakened,
and you accept. It is normal to accept
what already, like history,
is immutable.

Such is poetry without invention,
invented in advance in your person.
You are the truth and its words,
calling it the poem you thought
you could not write.

Forever

I do know that birds continue to live and procreate as long as the weather is amenable and the food there—as if it were a deal between the weather and the crops. No questions asked. And the birds are in earnest, as I am in seeking a reason for their lives, for what reason I myself do not understand. I, too, in my way, am ignorant of my self, my purpose—to perform simply the role of questioner?

If I were to say it is because I want to know—I will carry out my function, as the birds carry out theirs.

I must call it good, because to deny it is not one of my purposes, or is it? And here I am asking a question once again, meditating on the practically nothing, finding something to say about it, this that I have written, for the sake of living with questions forever.

The Form

The form falls in on itself,
its identity broken. There
on the bare ground the pieces
crawl toward each other.

For Jane Kenyon

As I die, it will be to feel myself
leaving a world on its way
to accomplish its own purpose.

It is in my nature to think so,
in the nature of things themselves.

If I Should

fall asleep forever
I will have lived the inevitable
life of dying. But I am awakened
and involved in feeling once again,
alive to my emotions, caring
that I feel, loving the moment.

It is good to be back
for a time
between happiness and dread.

Once Upon a Time

Once upon a time there was an animal that did not think it was worth the effort to get up from its lair to go out in search of food. It would only be repeating itself, as it had been doing day after day since it was born, and so it would try to ignore this routine self and instead stay put and dream of excitements it could not find in the course of the day. It closed its eyes, snuggled into itself and fell asleep to dream and dreamt that it was growing hungry and would soon rise and go in search of food and then it dreamt of resisting this need. It awoke, annoyed with itself.

The Bearer of Pain

We come back to the source of our pain.
It is pain that cannot exceed itself
and so there is comfort
but we return because it is
reassuring to have survived in pain,
the measure of our success
for as long as it takes to live
and be known
as the bearer of pain.

Myself

I am alone with my anger,
I can knock a hole in it
by knocking on someone's door
and keeping a smile
as I respond to questions
from behind the door.

It opens
and I am tremulous
with pleasure
in the presence of a stranger.

The Journey

A dog running in the shadow of trees—
I felt its loneliness and ran with it
in my thoughts. I wished for the dog
a quick death, if it had to be,
without its knowing it happening.

The dog was running steadily
when suddenly I heard it bark
and a bark respond. I write
to let you know, to cheer with me
at its journey.

SECTION FOUR

Because

Because of the sun on my face,
I have forgotten what it was
I wanted to complain about,
and now that I am bathed in warmth
I am not the person I remember
but a while past, and because
I have forgotten myself in the sun
I take my identity from its rays
and my life from its heat
and my beliefs from its glow.

When the sun sinks
beneath the horizon I will carry on
with what I have been given
to survive until it returns:
I am its agent and its power.

The Marmoset

I feed an ancestor out of my hand.
Does he know who I am?
He stops suddenly to look up at me.

Perhaps placing his nose in my palm
is to let me know of the relationship
I honor, with my hand outstretched.

Forget It

That a dog should see another dog and trot over to it—that can only mean they have a sense of their own identity. Would a man seeing another man walk over to him? Forget it.

Of course I've heard of dogs barking at each other and tearing at each other's throats. This happens among men too, but when they are friendly—I mean dog to dog—nothing stops them from getting together. Imagine two men—presume they are strangers—approaching each other like two lost friends, embracing and talking over the beauty and naturalness of being men, as dogs do with one another. Forget it.

And here I am even doubting that my fellow men will, on reading this, call out—I really wouldn't mind if it were a woman. I would myself prefer it, and for her to say, "Why don't we cling to each other in a world where the stars are so far apart from us?"

We

I

You lift your face to mine
with the sweet, sad expression
of the life of reservation
toward delight in love
of moments long ago that left
their impress on your thoughts
and I gaze back with love
newly acquired in old age
and the sadness that is mine
of love so long delayed
in coming meets yours
long languishing in fear.

II

We are fading apart,
each in a cloud of physicians
growing dense. I am awake,
it seems, simply to record
this moment in our long life
together of words shared
face to face and dined to.

Even so, we knew of the end,
and I am most happy to forget
myself in you, that sense

I take with me
and walk and sleep with
as in a tent shielding me
from the bad weather
of separation.

It Moves Me to Love You,

what I might have lost
by merging our identity,
to lose that love of you
in losing love of self
I do not love in being self
alone.

An Apology

I placed a chair between my desk
and bookcase and there it stands
vacant, without having been sat in
all the years since.

Who could have imagined
it would not be sat in
in all this time? I'm so sorry
for something made useless
to itself.

The Door

Wherever I go I carry the door with me, opened or closed, depending on what's happening. In the event I am attending a party of friends I've known since childhood, the door remains half open. In the event I attend a meeting to discuss the latest political upset, the door is totally closed, but I have an ear pressed to it, in case I hear something extraordinary.

In the event I attend a luncheon for business purposes, such as to obtain a grant, the door remains open. However, the person who is seated opposite me across the desk will not find me at the open door at all. I'll be down the corridor, hidden in a corner, but he'll hear me.

And so, though carrying the door may be an inconvenience and tiring, if not somewhat bizarre, I'm prepared to defend it as a perfectly normal procedure, and should you see me straining to carry it, you could, if you would, lend a hand, putting your pity at rest by putting it to work. Thank you.

Fact

I'm closing the door,
I don't expect to find happiness
behind it, communicating with myself.

The idea is to be able to say
I'm going to close the door
and then close it.

Christmas Eve

Smitty, the cop in the booth
at the intersection of two converging streets,
waved us over on Christmas Eve. It was
a silent deserted night. He was standing
in the entrance, holding out a plate,
on it slices of a Christmas pie. Each of us
accepted a slice, thanking him hastily.
My friends gobbled theirs. I held mine,
looking down on it, wanting to eat it.

Smitty, I told myself, was not trying
to convert me to his observances of Christmas,
which I feared, hearing my parents talking
between them as Jews. I was not aware
of the religion of my friends.
It never occurred to either of us to ask.

They gobbled their slices with great relish,
with throaty sounds. If they were Jews,
they were abandoning their identity. I was
sorry for myself in such confusion.
It was not worth the anguish
of losing my friends if as Jews
they were breaking with their beliefs.

I held my slice with thumb and forefinger,
scarcely touching the edge, and slowly
lifted it to my mouth. I tried to assure myself
that it was only to discover the taste.

It was sweet. Still, with misgivings,
I nibbled a piece of the crust and swallowed.
I bit off a much larger chunk, with apple in it,
and soon finished the whole with pleasure,
feeling betrayed in myself.

At home, later that night, I did not tell
my parents. I let them be gentle with me,
as always, and I was gentle in return. It was
Christian of Smitty to have done what he did.
It was Christian of me to accept the slice.
I could thank him as a Jew.

For Johannes Edfelt

I once had a religion to turn to.
I listen to a singer singing
the prayer I once sang.

What I have now is myself,
the skeptic,
looking at trees and grass
that live out their lives
never in doubt.

My childhood is in that song.
In contentment with my childhood,
I look skyward with curiosity.

For Rose

1913–1995

I have a name
a substitute
for the word
infinity.

When my name is called
it is not me
you are calling.

UNIVERSITY PRESS OF NEW ENGLAND publishes under its own imprint and is the publisher for Brandeis University Press, Dartmouth College, Middlebury College Press, University of New Hampshire, Tufts University, Wesleyan University Press, and Salzburg Seminar.

ABOUT THE AUTHOR

David Ignatow has published sixteen volumes of poetry and three prose collections. Born in Brooklyn, he has lived most of his life in the New York metropolitan area, at various times working as editor of *The American Poety Review* and the *Beloit Poety Journal*, poetry editor of *The Nation*, and co-editor of *Chelsea*. He has taught at Columbia, the New School for Social Research, the University of Kentucky, the University of Kansas, York College of the City University of New York, New York University, and Vassar College.

The National Institute of Arts and Letters has presented to Mr. Ignatow an award "for a lifetime of creative effort." His work has been recognized also with the Bollingen Prize, two Guggenheim Fellowships, the Wallace Stevens fellowship from Yale University, the Rockefeller Foundation fellowship, the Poety Society of America's Shelley Memorial Award, and an award from the National Endowment for the Arts. He is president emeritus of the Poetry Society of America and a member of the executive board of the Walt Whitman Birthplace Association, Huntington, Long Island. His home is in East Hampton, Long Island.

His most recent books are *Shadowing the Ground* (1991) and *Against the Evidence: Selected Poems* 1934-1994 (1994).

LIBRARY OF CONGRESS CATALOGING-IN-PUBLICATION DATA

Ingnatow, David, 1914–
    I Have a Name   /   David Ignatow.
    p.   cm.—(Wesleyan poetry)
    ISBN 0–8195–2232–5 (alk. paper).—ISBN 0–8195–2240–6 (alk. paper)
    I. Title. II. Series
PS3517.G5312   1996
811'.54—dc20   96–19350